15 HOUSE-PLANTS EVEN YOU CAN'T KILL

JOE ELDER

With photographs by the author

BERKLEY BOOKS, NEW YORK

15 HOUSEPLANTS EVEN YOU CAN'T KILL

A Berkley Book / published by arrangement with
the author

PRINTING HISTORY
Berkley trade paperback edition / October 1984
Berkley mass market edition / June 1991

ISBN: 0-425-13130-0

A BERKLEY BOOK ® TM 757,375
Berkley Books are published by The Berkley Publishing Group,
200 Madison Avenue, New York, New York 10016.
The name "BERKLEY" and the "B" logo are
trademarks belonging to Berkley Publishing Corporation.

PRINTED IN THE UNITED STATES OF AMERICA

10 9 8 7 6 5 4 3

CONTENTS

PREFACE

If you're anything like me, houseplants don't loom large on your list of life's major priorities. Yes, they're attractive enough and they look good in other people's homes or offices, but grow them yourself? The idea sounds about as appealing as a session of root canal surgery.

On the other hand, if you're also like me, you probably wouldn't mind having a few of those leafy green things hanging around as a backdrop to your fascinating personal or business life. They really don't look half bad. What gives you pause is that having them and caring for them are two very different matters.

You probably know an avid home gardener whose windows look like miniature jungles. Admit it, you may even, in a weak moment, have felt a twinge of envy toward that person. Of course, it was a mild twinge. Let's be honest about it: You don't actually want to do much of anything for your indoor greenery.

Until now, you've probably never even opened a book on

growing houseplants. Well, I have good news for you: You still haven't opened a book on growing houseplants. Personally, I never *grow* them, but I've learned through trial and error how to keep them alive and looking reasonably good with an absolute minimum of effort. What more can you ask of a houseplant?

Since I have not yet perfected a system of *total* neglect, I must caution you that there are two basic things your plants really do need: light and water. Give them these two ingredients, and only these ingredients, in reasonable proportions, and your plants will fare very well indeed. Simplistic though it may sound, this advice is the basis of all houseplant survival.

I can tell you how to maintain fifteen houseplants, no more and no less. If there is a sixteenth lurking out there somewhere, I haven't found it. In fact, I'm sure it doesn't exist. Here, then, are *the* fifteen, rock-bottom, all-time indestructible houseplants that need little sun, less water, and no love at all—the fifteen houseplants that even you can't kill.

Part One:
BASIC CARE AND FEEDING

Attitude

There is only one attitude that makes any sense where house-plants are concerned. That attitude is called *benign neglect*. Embrace it, cultivate it, never forget it. Some of my plants have survived downright abuse, although I don't actually advocate that approach. What I do say is this: Don't pamper your plants. Contrary to a popular current notion, plants are not at all like people. They do not require tender loving care.

We all know some well-intentioned eccentric who indulges his or her plants, who strokes them, communicates with their auras, and even (God forbid!) talks to them. Whether the plants ever talk back is generally not known. If they could, I suspect their owners would get an earful of unprintable Plantese.

The fact is, houseplants—and especially my fifteen, of course—are much tougher than they are given credit for. They don't need much of anything. My fifteen will adapt remarkably well to a variety of conditions. You don't have to become a horticultural guru to keep them alive and kicking. Nor do you have to develop a green thumb, or any other kind of thumb, for that matter.

4

When confidence falters, remember ELDER'S FIRST LAW: THUMBS ARE FOR PUSHING IN TACKS, NOT FOR GROWING HOUSEPLANTS.

Hand in hand with benign neglect in the attitude department is the concept of Less is More. If you hover over your plants like an anxious parent, if you feel constantly that you must Do Something for them, you will wind up with spoiled plants. What's worse, you will defeat the whole purpose of this book.

Sources

The best source of houseplants is clever friends who know how to propagate them from their own plants. I know *you* don't want to propagate plants, but why not take advantage of those foolish souls who do? Of course, the freebies must be on my approved list. Otherwise, they will probably wither and die before you reach your doorstep.

If you're going to part with hard-earned cash, be cautious in buying plants directly from a greenhouse. Greenhouses are artificial jungles with bountiful light, warmth, and humidity. Plants in greenhouses look like props from a Tarzan movie, but take them out of this paradise and into your dark, arid, dusty, overheated living room and they may go into shock and drop half their leaves. Be sure your greenhouse plants are well-wrapped in brown paper before you take them out into the cold, and keep them in a warm place for several days.

Greenhouses that have florist shops attached, where plants have adjusted to halfway normal (i.e., homelike) conditions, are safer. So are those giant plant warehouses or even discount stores like K-Mart, where greenery is sold by the acre and often at very reasonable prices.

I've bought some of my best plants in five and dime stores. A plant that can exist in a Woolworth's basement is a plant after my own heart, a true survivor.

Which plant to buy? Of course, it will be among my elite

fifteen. Beyond that, you obviously should seek out a healthy-looking plant, one that is green and fresh and full. If it has a lot of bare stems or yellow leaves, and especially if you see something crawling on it—eschew!

Pots

Plants invariably come in one of two things—a clay pot or a plastic pot. Of the two, the former is usually to be preferred. Your basic, terra-cotta clay pot is a classic. Supposedly it "breathes" (we won't concern ourselves over exactly how that works), and its timeless beauty makes it fit into any home or office decor.

Plastic pots, on the other hand, often have plantlike things, like twining leaves or flowers, embossed on them, come in a dreary shade of dark green, and, let's face it, are somewhat tacky. They do have a few advantages, however. The plain white ones aren't that bad looking, and they are light in weight and therefore useful as so-called hanging baskets. Since hanging baskets usually contain bushy trailing plants, you fortunately don't have to see much of the plastic. If your *standing* pot is made of plastic, you can always hide it in a wicker basket, a ceramic planter, or whatever.

Don't waste precious time or energy worrying about containers. Unless you're decorating model rooms at Bloomingdale's, you can usually make do very well with the container your plant comes in.

Light

Once you get your plant home, you will be faced with the burning question of where to put it. Near a window, to be sure, but which window, you may well ask. Actually, almost any bright window will do for my fifteen survivors except one that gets direct sun all day long.

Don't put your plant *too* close to the window. It might well be cold and drafty there in the winter. Try to set the plant back about a foot so the leaves aren't touching the glass. If you're hanging a plant from the ceiling, set the hook or bracket back far enough from the window so that the leaves don't touch the pane.

Plants do thrive on bright light, but my fifteen will tolerate a lot less than most. I'll give you more specific parameters for each in the section on the plants themselves—they're much wider than you might think. The same plant that goes bananas in a bay window with several hours of morning sun might also at least survive handily in a dim corner.

Windows face in the usual four directions. The southern exposure gets the most sun, but that tends to burn or dry up most plants. We will save that exposure for cactus, which thrives on arid, desertlike conditions. A good, strong north light is excellent for all the plants in this book. East with a couple of hours of morning sun is better yet. West is very good, too, though it might prove a bit torrid for some plants during the hot summer months.

Along with light, we must add a word about temperature. Volumes have been written about the ideal temperatures for houseplants, and the volumes often disagree. What they usually fail to note is that plants adapt in their own fashion to the environment in which they're placed. They may have a few initial adjustment problems—wilting and drooping or dropping leaves for a spell—but most will finally settle down and do what they're supposed to do—namely, absolutely nothing but exist for your pleasure and convenience. It would be a full-time job to try to create the perfect home environment for every plant, and you wouldn't be reading this book if you wanted to get into that scene. If you feel comfortable with the temperature—reasonably warm during the day, cooler when you go to bed at night—so will your plant. If it doesn't, it had bloody well better get used to it.

Most plants are phototropic, which means they tend to grow toward the light. The only thing you need to know about phototropism is that you ought to rotate your plants occasionally so they won't get lopsided. If you like lopsided plants, then don't rotate them. It won't hurt the plants, though it doesn't say much for your taste.

Water

Nothing seems to provoke more anxiety among plant owners than watering. It all stems (we might as well get that pun over with) from the compulsive need most neophyte plant owners seem to have to play Mommy or Daddy to their plants. I can't emphasize enough that you don't have to do much of anything for them. When in doubt, recall ELDER'S SECOND LAW: IF YOU WANT TO BE A MOTHER HEN, RAISE CHICKENS, NOT PLANTS.

More plants have doubtless been killed by overwatering than any other factor. This is quite literally a case of killing with kindness, but who ever said you have to be kind to plants? Remember this about watering: When in doubt, don't.

How much water? How often? I reduce these questions to a simple formula that anybody can cope with. Water twice a week, thoroughly on Saturday and lightly on Wednesday. (If you insist on Sunday and Thursday, or Monday and Friday, have it your way.)

How thorough is thorough? Until the water runs out of the hole in the bottom of the pot or spills out into the saucer attached to the bottom of the hanging basket. (You'll soon get the hang of it, to dispose of our other obligatory plant pun.) Pour off the excess water from the saucer and you've completed your major watering of the week. Don't even think about buying plants with containers that have no hole: They are major candidates for death by drowning.

How light is light? That's a little harder to answer, since, this time, you don't want the water to run out of the hole. (However, don't panic if it does; you haven't done any irreparable harm.) You'll find that you need about half as much water on Wednesday as you did on Saturday. If you gave the plant, let's say, two cups of water on Saturday, then you'll probably need about one on Wednesday. You'll quickly develop a feel for its needs.

The point is to keep the soil evenly moist all the time. It should feel slightly damp to the touch—and touching is the best way to gauge the need for water. If your kids start making mud pies with the soil, you've gone too far. If it looks like the Gobi Desert, you haven't gone far enough. Better to let the soil dry out a little between waterings, however, than to overwater.

Two other pointers about watering that you must heed:
- Water plants in the morning.
- Use tepid or room-temperature water.

If you feel compelled to ask why, you're reading the wrong book.

All plant authorities stress the need for humidity. My fifteen survivors like humidity as much as any other plants, but they will not shrivel up without it. As with temperature, they tend to adapt to the conditions you give them in your home or office. If you liked to play with water pistols as a kid, you might want to spray your plants occasionally. I use an old, well-rinsed Windex bottle filled with tepid water, and spray when the mood strikes me, which admittedly isn't often. You must not spray on rainy or very humid days. Otherwise, spraying is good for the plants and good therapy for you.

Like everything else around the house, plants collect dust, and so, perhaps once or twice a year, it makes sense to give your plants a shower. Unless they're trees, you can literally hold them under the shower or kitchen spray (again, use tepid water) for a minute or two. With the broad-leafed species, just wipe off the leaves with a damp sponge or paper towel. Which leads me to ELDER'S THIRD LAW: PLANTS ARE LIKE FURNITURE; WHEN YOU CAN WRITE YOUR NAME ON THEM, IT'S TIME TO CLEAN.

Feeding

There are two schools of thought about feeding, or fertilizing, houseplants: Do and don't. I would probably be drummed out of a horticultural society (if any would have me in the first place) for saying so, but if you don't want to get into feeding your plants, forget about it. Most of them will do well enough for several years without additional nutrients.

There is no denying, however, that plants will do even better if you do feed them. If you must, the simplest method is to use those little fertilizer spikes or tabs, for sale at any plant or garden center, that you just stick in the soil and forget about. They slowly release their chemicals over a period of several weeks or even months depending on the brand.

If you want to get fancy and use liquid or water-soluble fertilizers, be sure to use them at half the strength recommended on the packages, and half as often.

Don't fertilize your plants in the winter, when they don't do much growing anyway. Feed only from about March through October. Or, to come full circle, don't feed at all.

Pinching and Pruning

Let us not dwell on these somewhat arcane horticultural techniques. As with feeding, you may or may not do them, as you choose. Your plants will survive either way.

Pinching means literally to pinch off (between your thumb

and index finger) the terminal or last bud on the stem of a plant. This tends to stop that stem from growing longer and forces growth out of the sides of the stem in the form of new branching and leaves. Pruning is a bit more radical, something like a haircut. It means to cut back the plant all over to whatever size and shape you want it to assume. In either event, the result is often a fuller-looking, healthier plant.

If your plants start to look a bit leggy, as a few of them, such as Philodendron and Devil's Ivy, may eventually look, be brave and take the pruning and pinching plunge. If you're the type who enjoys picking lint off other people's dark clothes, you'll probably find pinching especially gratifying. In most cases, however, you'll never have to indulge in either activity.

Bugs and Blights

Scale, mealy bugs, aphids, red spider mites, white flies, mildew, slugs, worms—the very names strike terror in the hearts of dedicated home gardeners. Happily, however, *we* are not dedicated home gardeners. How liberating to know that we don't have to *care* about diseases and plant pests!

I have tried manfully to cope with some of the above plagues, with no success at all. It is almost impossible, first of all, to tell which disease you are dealing with. Those little suckers are usually visible only under a microscope (and none too attractive even if you're able to spot one). The cure can be just as bad as the disease, assuming you can figure out which cure to employ. Sprays may leave ugly residues on your plants, may burn the leaves and, worse, may pollute your atmosphere with dangerous chemicals that leave you gagging.

If you bought a reasonably healthy looking plant in the first place, and if you're giving it adequate light and water, it's probably not going to be assaulted by aphids, anyway. Plant diseases are not all that common in the home. However, if your plant is obviously a candidate for that Big Greenhouse in

11

the Sky—and you'll know it when the leaves start shriveling and wrinkling and then dropping like rain, and nothing you do seems to help—then let it go, trash it, and don't look back.

If that sounds heartless, so be it. After all, we benign neglectors can have *no* heart where plants are concerned. We must be pragmatic about these terminal matters. If you've had a couple of years' use out of your five- or ten-dollar plant, what is there to complain about? As long as you haven't been foolish enough to fall in love with a plant, you should have no problem disposing of it. If you find yourself weakening, you must bring to mind ELDER'S FOURTH LAW: LIFE IS TOO SHORT TO WASTE ON A FICKLE FATSIA.

Part Two:
THE PLANTS

ALUMINUM PLANT

It's interesting to note how many of my Fabulous Fifteen even *sound* as tough as they are: Screw Pine, Spider Plant, Snake Plant, Arrowhead Plant, and this one, Aluminum Plant. The Aluminum Plant comes from Vietnam, of all places. If it has survived that benighted land all these centuries, you can be sure it will have no trouble coping with your home or office.

The Aluminum Plant usually remains fairly small, perhaps a foot or a tad more in height, and quite bushy. The leaves are oblong in shape, with slightly saw-toothed edges. They have a quilted texture, and the raised parts are blotched as if with silvery, or aluminum, paint.

There seems to be some confusion among the "authorities" as to what to do with the Aluminum Plant, but it's really quite easy: Do as little as possible.

Light

Keep this plant in bright indirect light. A northern exposure is best, but a little morning sun would be welcome. A lot of afternoon sun would not. The Aluminum Plant is very phototropic, so do rotate it to keep the shape symmetrical if that sort of thing is important to you. It will do well in average home or office temperatures.

Water

Water twice a week, and keep the soil evenly damp. If the Aluminum Plant dries out, you'll know it. The plant will not only wilt, it will totally collapse and look like a candidate for the compost heap. Water it thoroughly, however, and it should spring back to attention. Spray the leaves as often as you think of it.

Special Tips

The Aluminum Plant is either a fast grower or a slow grower, depending upon which books you read. The ones I've had have tended to grow fast, and yours probably will, too. Eventually they get to look rather leggy, so don't hesitate to prune back if that happens. This will only help to keep the plant looking bushy and compact. Fertilize, if you will, throughout the spring and summer.

ARROWHEAD
PLANT

This Central American native is variously called Nephthytis and Syngonium in reference books, but I call it plain old Arrowhead Plant. (Never buy a houseplant whose name you can't spell.)

This is a *great* plant for dark places, an absolute basic among the all-time fifteen. It not only survives in that dim corner, it grows! The Arrowhead Plant often shows up in those abominations that florists call dish gardens, low planters containing several totally unrelated specimens. If the Arrowhead Plant can get along in that mixed company, it will certainly get along with you.

The single green leaves are shaped like—you guessed it— arrowheads. They may be three to eight inches long, and have markings of white, cream, silver, or yellow. There are also tri-leafed varieties. You can let the leaves droop or (to achieve larger leaves) train them up a piece of bark or a trellis. If you're doing your job of neglecting benignly, you'll let them droop.

Light

The Arrowhead Plant will thrive in any kind of light except full-time sun. Typical home or office temperatures are satisfactory.

Water

Give your Arrowhead Plant the usual twice-a-week dousing. The soil should remain moist but not soggy. Spray or shower if you get the urge.

Special Tips

If, in a moment of madness, you feel really ambitious, you can grow Arrowhead Plants in plain water. Select a few long shoots, trim off any leaves that would be below the water line, and pop them in water in any attractive container. They look especially good in clear glass. Throw in a handful of charcoal, which you can get anywhere plants are sold, and change the water every month or so. The plants will root and last indefinitely.

I mention this esoteric activity only because the Arrowhead Plant is so easy and undemanding that there is really nothing special to say about it.

BABY'S TEARS

Despite its delicate name, Baby's Tears is tough as nails and among the very easiest plants to keep looking good. With even casual care, you can hardly hold it back.

Baby's Tears grows naturally on the islands of Corsica and Sardinia, so it is not strictly speaking a tropical plant. Like other plants from semi-tropical or temperate areas of the world, it seems to adapt more easily to the home than true tropicals, with their greater demands for warmth and humidity.

This is a creeper, a low-growing, spreading plant with thousands of tiny leaves and stems that intertwine to form a bright green mound. Baby's Tears doesn't achieve any height to speak of, but it will soon fill any container and spill over the sides.

Light

Give your Baby's Tears strong, bright light with little or no direct sun. A north window is ideal, but east or west, with a

few hours of sun per day, would be satisfactory, too. Average room temperatures are fine, but I've let my Baby's Tears winter over in a summer house with minimal heat (temperatures in the fifties) with no dire consequences. They have also survived weeks of summer temperatures in the nineties.

Water

Because this plant grows in bogs in nature, it thrives on moisture. This is one plant that will even tolerate soggy soil for a while. Give it a thorough watering (remember, until the water runs out of the hole), and check midweek to see if it needs more. If the soil feels dry to the touch, give it another splash of water. If it doesn't, don't.

Special Tips

If the plant gets too dry, you'll soon know it. It will flatten out like a green pancake. In that case, give it a thorough watering and it'll soon perk up. If any leaves dry out and turn brown, which they will, just snip them off with a pair of scissors. Baby's Tears doesn't need much feeding. It will probably last for several years without it. If you want to feed, do so in the spring. You can easily trim your plant back with scissors if it gets out of hand, or out of pot. If you want to do nothing but give your Baby's Tears the recommended light and water, this plant won't quit.

CACTUS

Everyone knows the Cactus. It is what comic cowboys always land on when thrown by their horses; it is what parched prospectors and their burros derive water from; and it is what photographers always silhouette against garish desert sunsets. As a houseplant, it is also about as foolproof as they come.

There are literally hundreds of kinds of Cacti, all of them native to the New World. Most grow in arid, desertlike regions, but some, like the familiar Christmas Cactus, are found in tropical rain forests. The latter require rather tricky care at home, so we shall certainly not deal with them here. The desert varieties, however, all need the same amount of attention, which is to say almost no attention at all.

Light

At last, we have a plant that does best in full sun. It is the only one that I can completely recommend for that southern

exposure. This is not to say that it won't grow in partial sun; it just won't grow quite as well. Cactus will even survive for a long time in bright north light with no sun at all. If you happen to give your Cactus sunny days and cool nights (forties and fifties) in the winter, it may produce spectacular flowers in the spring. Placing the Cactus close to (but not touching) a cold window actually helps to bring about this result, but don't count on it. Unlike pet poodles, plants are not eager to please. It follows, of course, that you should not be eager to please *them*.

Water

Cactus is the camel of the plant kingdom. It really does store up water, and therefore needs very little from you, thank you. Water thoroughly but no more than once a week in spring and summer, once a *month* in fall and winter. Always let Cactus dry out between waterings. Too much water tends to rot the Cactus and eventually will turn it into an oozing green blob. This is not advisable unless you are producing science fiction movies.

Special Tips

You surely don't need to be told not to touch the Cactus. Those little spines hurt and are difficult to remove from your skin. If you want to dust the plant, give it a blast with a hair dryer. If you fertilize, once a year, in the spring, is adequate. And if you travel a lot and like something green and undemanding to be waiting for you at home, you need look no further than the Cactus.

CHINESE EVERGREEN

Surprise, surprise, the Chinese Evergreen does indeed come from China, along with such other exotic places as Sri Lanka, Malaysia, and Borneo. It's another one of those indispensable forget-about-it plants. Give it nothing but a little light and water, and it will perform admirably for you. Every teller in my bank has one reposing on the counter, which should tell you something about this plant's durability.

There are several varieties of Chinese Evergreen, the basic green one and others with leaves splotched in white, cream, or silver. The heart or sword-shaped leaves, on canelike stems, may be six inches to one foot in length, and the plant may grow up to three feet tall. Some varieties look rather like the common Dieffienbachia, which, for reasons we won't dwell on here, didn't make our list of the favored fifteen.

Chinese Evergreens are often cultivated in just plain water, where they last forever and look quite exotic.

Light

In nature a dweller of the jungle floor, where it receives filtered light, the Chinese Evergreen needs little light in the home. It will do best in a bright north window with average home temperatures, but it will do adequately almost anywhere except in all-day sun. It's a natural for your proverbial dim corner.

Water

The usual twice-a-week watering is all that need concern you. In fact, you may find that one main watering is sufficient, particularly if the plant is not receiving much light. (There is doubtless a scientific reason for this, but does anyone really care?) Do sponge off the leaves if and when the mood strikes you.

Special Tips

I can't think of a one. If you're interested in growing the Chinese Evergreen in water, the technique has already been amply documented under special tips for the Arrowhead Plant.

CORN PLANT

Of all the *dracaenas* (and there are many members of the genus), the Corn Plant seems to me the most rugged. It grows and grows on moderate light and water, and unlike some of its *dracaenas* cousins, it thoughtfully doesn't drop its lower leaves. It also needs little feeding and is happy in the same pot for years. If you want a handsome plant that grows as high as an elephant's eye, the Corn Plant is for you.

The leaves of the Corn Plant do indeed look like corn. Sprouting off a canelike stem, they are broad and arching, either plain deep green or green striped with yellow (or yellow striped with green, if that's your perception). The plant grows slowly, but, oh, does it grow! It may experience some dormant periods when it doesn't seem to be moving at all, but then it takes off like old Jack's beanstalk, to which it bears more than a passing resemblance. Make no mistake about it, this one will hit the ceiling if conditions are halfway decent.

For a native of tropical Africa, the Corn Plant adapts amazingly well to home and office.

29

Light

A little sun (east or west window) is okay, but I find that the Corn Plant does best in a bright north window. If you want to set it back a few feet from that window, it may grow a bit slower. Average home and office temperatures are acceptable, too.

Water

At the risk of sounding like a broken record, give the Corn Plant your usual two waterings per week. Keep the soil just damp, never soggy. Those broad leaves might be wiped off or sprayed occasionally if you are so inclined.

Special Tips

If you're going to feed the Corn Plant, do it in the spring and again in late summer, no more than that. You don't want this plant growing *too* fast, or it may make a U-turn at the ceiling and head toward the floor. The Corn Plant, otherwise, requires very little special attention, which of course is precisely how a plant should behave.

DEVIL'S IVY (POTHOS)

Devil's Ivy is a cornerstone in any collection of indestructible houseplants. It always looks good, needs no special attention, and lets you simply relax and forget about it, which is what any self-respecting houseplant should do.

Devil's Ivy is native to the Solomon Islands, where we are told it grows on the bark of trees and produces enormous leaves up to two feet long. It will do no such thing for you, but it does have attractive heart-shaped leaves that may reach several inches in length. They look something like those of the common Philodendron but are usually a lighter shade of green and blotched with yellow or cream.

Devil's Ivy is often called Pothos but is really a *Scindapsus*, for whatever that is worth. A common variety is also called Marble Queen.

This plant is often sold growing vinelike up a piece of bark. I prefer it trailing in a hanging basket, though the leaves do grow larger the other way. You can also cut off stems and grow them in plain water.

Light

Devil's Ivy does best in a bright, warm place. A north window or an east window, where the plant gets morning sun only, would be excellent locations. I kept one several feet from a window in a darkish corner for years, however, and it fared quite well. If you can't give it perfect light, give it dim. The only drawback is that dim light will cause the plant to lose its variegated colors.

Water

Devil's Ivy should almost dry out between waterings. Give it one thorough watering (remember, until the water comes out the hole) on Saturday and a very skimpy midweek splash. Spraying and showering will help to keep the plant fresh and colorful but are not essential to its survival.

Special Tips

Use fertilizer spikes in the spring if you wish. This is one of the very few plants in this book that will benefit from pinching and pruning. Mind you, you don't have to do these things, but they will help to keep the plant healthy and bushy. If your Devil's Ivy is in a hanging basket, at least cut back all the stems a few inches in the spring. Don't—repeat, don't—let them grow as long as clotheslines and wind them around your curtain rods.

FATSIA

It's Latin name is *Fatsia japonica*, which, as you might well guess, means that the plant comes from Japan. There, it is an outdoor, evergreen shrub that may grow to fifteen feet. The Fatsia also has a Chinese cousin that is a prime source of rice paper (a bit of botanical trivia that you may want to drop at your next cocktail party).

This is one of the most popular houseplants, and deservedly so. Because it grows in temperate climates, it hangs tough indoors, where it makes a very striking impression. If you want a bold and dramatic plant that looks good in home or office, stop right here.

You will know the Fatsia by its distinctive foliage. Its leaves are a rich, glossy green in color and shaped somewhat like those of the maple tree. They may grow up to a foot across and the plant itself up to four feet or more.

The Fatsia was mated with the Irish Ivy to produce something called the Fatshedera, a similar plant that requires similar care.

As a hybrid, however, the Fatshedera does not qualify for placement on my all-time list. Only thoroughbreds need apply.

Light

Like many plants in this book, the Fatsia does best in semi-sunny places, preferably an east or west window, but it puts up quite well with poor light conditions, too. The only thing the Fatsia doesn't like is very warm temperatures. Definitely keep it away from radiators in the winter. It will do well even with temperatures in the fifties.

Water

Give the Fatsia its regular two waterings per week. The soil should stay just moist, never soggy. The broad leaves will look better if they are wiped off occasionally with a damp cloth.

Special Tips

A little fertilizer in the spring is helpful. If you live in an area where winters are mild, you may even grow the Fatsia outdoors.

GRAPE IVY

If you want a trailing plant that requires almost no care, the Grape Ivy is your baby. It hangs in profusion in every sidewalk cafe in Manhattan, coated, no doubt, in cooking fat and cigar smoke. Given a little basic light and water, it will turn handsprings for you.

This native of Northern South America and the West Indies is related to the grape family but is not an ivy. (Or is it the other way around? Does it matter?) Its three-part triangular leaves (not unlike those of Poison Ivy) are a dark metallic green on top, reddish and hairy underneath. The Grape Ivy, as noted, is a trailer, with curling tendrils that wrap themselves around anything in proximity, including you if you stand still long enough.

Light

If you have a bright spot where your Grape Ivy will get only a little direct sun, it will thrive. (Too much sun, if it doesn't dry out the plant, will result in a thicker, coarser-textured leaf.) But Grape Ivy is great for dimmer places, too. They seem to like the arid, fluorescent-lit atmosphere of an office, where I've seen many a robust specimen. Average home temperatures are desirable, but for a tropical plant, the Grape Ivy is remarkably adaptable to coolness. Mine has wintered over in the fifties (the temperature range, not the decade) with no serious problems.

Water

Water twice a week for best results, but don't lose sleep if you forget once in a while. "They" say the soil shouldn't dry out completely, but I haven't found this to be harmful on occasion. Do spray the leaves if you get off on that sort of thing.

Special Tips

The Grape Ivy is spectacularly *un*special in its requirements. Fertilizer spikes, used as directed, are doubtless beneficial, but your Grape Ivy will serve its time for at least a couple of years without them.

PHILODENDRON

The most interesting thing about the Philodendron is that it was "discovered" in Jamaica and brought to England by Captain Bligh of *Bounty* fame. Other than that, it is surely the most familiar, the most ubiquitous, the most boring plant in captivity. (One is tempted to call it Bligh's revenge for the mutiny.) The Philodendron was the first tropical plant to "make it big" in America back in the Depression, and five and dimes are still chock-a-block with them.

On the other hand, if you want a really durable plant that you don't have to think about (what other kind is there?), the Philodendron is just the thing. There are countless varieties, but the one we're talking about is the very popular trailer with plain green, heart-shaped leaves. In florist's shops, it is often sold growing up a piece of bark and coated with some waxy substance that makes the leaves look as if they would glow in the dark. The leaves do tend to grow larger if trained to climb on something (the name Philodendron means "tree-loving"),

but if you must have this plant, the ones that come in hanging baskets at least look more natural.

Light

It doesn't matter where you put the Philodendron as long as it isn't in full sun. A little morning sun would not be amiss, but a bright north window with average home temperatures would be ideal. You can even put a Philodendron on a mantle or bookshelf away from the window, where it should at least survive for quite a long time. Of course, the leaves will grow smaller and smaller in dim light, but you can't have everything.

Water

If you're the type who is apt to forget to water your plants (and we hope you are), you and the Philodendron were made for each other. Give it the usual biweekly watering if you think of it, and keep the soil just moist, but nothing dire will happen if you let the soil dry out occasionally. If you keep your Philodendron in dim light, it may well need only one watering per week. Spraying and showering will help to keep the plant fresh-looking.

Special Tips

For those bleeding hearts among you who care, do fertilize in spring and summer, and do pinch and prune for a bushier plant. If leaves turn yellow, and some invariably will, just snip them off; this, too, will induce new growth.

RUBBER PLANT

The Rubber Plant belongs to the fig family, of all things, but don't expect it to produce figs. This is the old-fashioned India Rubber Plant of Victorian parlors. If it survived in those dim, cheerless places, just imagine how it will perform for you. Until better plants were found in Brazil, it was a major source of rubber.

The leaves of the Rubber Plant are as familiar as those of any houseplant. Large (up to twelve inches in length), stiff, shiny, and waxy, they unfurl from red, spiky buds. They are usually plain dark green, but there are rarer, multicolored varieties.

Like its cousin, the less dependable Weeping Fig, the Rubber Plant can grow to tree-size in your home or office. It may need some pruning to keep it in its place, which of course is where any plant should be kept.

Light

The Rubber Plant responds best to some sun (an east or west window would be ideal) but will also do well in bright north light or even dimmer. The plant may drop leaves if placed in too cold a location. Average room temperatures are best.

Water

Give your Rubber Plant a thorough watering once a week and a very light watering, if any, midweek. The Rubber Plant can almost dry out between waterings. Too much water will result in yellowing, dropping leaves, but you'd have to submerge this plant to do it in. The leaves are so broad they almost demand an occasional swipe with a clean, damp cloth. If that sounds too much like work, forget the whole thing.

Special Tips

Unless you want a monster on your hands, don't go overboard with the feeding of a Rubber Plant. A few fertilizer spikes in the spring should be sufficient. Prune if necessary, and don't be surprised by the white goo that oozes out where you cut. Remember, they actually did make rubber out of this stuff once upon a time. For a healthier, bushier plant, you can pinch off some of the red buds, especially in the spring, when the plant is producing a lot of them.

SCREW PINE

The Screw Pine sounds tough and it is. There is virtually nothing short of blow-torching that you can do to kill it. It will withstand poor light, minimal water, no fertilizer, and long vacations by its owner.

This plant has nothing to do with pine trees, but, in its native habitat, it produces a fruit that looks like a pine cone. (Not to worry: It won't produce one for you.) Its long, sharply serrated leaves grow in spirals, corkscrew fashion, from a single stem: hence its name.

Screw Pines grow on the beaches of Polynesia, where it is said that their swordlike leaves caused no end of discomfort to our invading forces during World War II. Obviously, any plant that can impede an invasion of U.S. Marines has got to be good.

The Screw Pine is handsome and imposing. It will grow to three or four feet with green leaves, sometimes banded in creamy white, up to two feet long. It's a natural candidate for any low-humidity area, especially an office.

Light

The Screw Pine will tolerate virtually any light conditions. Several hours of sun per day would be ideal. Mine gets no sun at all in a bright north window, however, and just keeps rollin' along. If you relegate it to a dim corner, it may not produce much new growth, but it will survive and look respectable for a long time. Normal room temperatures are fine.

Water

The Screw Pine does need water, but sometimes it makes you wonder. I've abandoned mine for weeks during the summer with seemingly no ill effects. Give the Screw Pine a thorough watering once a week and skip the intermediate watering. This plant should dry out between waterings. Sponge off the leaves as you would make love to a porcupine—carefully!

Special Tips

Fertilizing in the spring isn't a bad idea, but too much feeding will cause the plant to grow too rapidly. The Screw Pine is naturally a slow grower. If its lower leaves turn brown and shrivel, just snip them off. Don't panic if your plant sends down aerial roots from the stem; it's not about to strangle your cat. In the wild, these help to anchor the Screw Pine to a windy beach, but at home you may safely ignore them.

SNAKE PLANT

This has got to be the all-time grand champion among un-killable houseplants. I've been trying to kill mine for years with no luck at all. Well, not actively trying, but with Snake Plants, one tends to carry benign neglect to extremes. Inasmuch as one can feel anything for a plant, this is the one you love to hate. Even its name sounds mean. It is also called mother-in-law plant. I don't know why, but it surely isn't a compliment.

Snake Plants are actually rather handsome in their austere way. They have tall, dark green spiky leaves that are usually streaked with paler green or yellow. They come from Africa, where they grow in harsh, dry conditions, so they can take anything you give (or deny) them.

Light

Don't even think about light where Snake Plants are concerned. You can put one in any kind of light in any window of the house and it will do splendidly. It will do best in strong light with some sun, but if you put it in a gloomy corner of the room, it will at least survive. Temperature is equally irrelevant. Mine has survived near freezing temperatures as well as several months of sitting on a hot radiator. (It did look good there.)

Water

Because of its desert background, the Snake Plant doesn't need much water. Water this one only once a week when you do your main watering. It doesn't seem to hurt a Snake Plant to dry out between waterings. Mine has gone waterless for several weeks at a time without any seeming ill effects. It is, therefore, one plant you never have to think about when you're on vacation.

Special Tips

There is almost nothing special one can, or indeed should, do for this plant. If you think of it, you might wash off the leaves with a damp paper towel once or twice a year. If an occasional leaf turns brown, just snip it off (or saw it off: this is a toughie). If the plant survives into old age—and it will, it will—the poor thing may reward your neglect, as mine has, with clusters of sweet-smelling white flowers.

SPIDER PLANT

SPIDER PLANT

If the Spider Plant were a Miss America contestant, it wouldn't win the crown, but it might well be chosen Miss Congeniality. It seems to be everybody's favorite houseplant. This is probably due to its habit of producing spidery little plantlets, or "babies" as they are dotingly called. I hold no truck with such sentimental twaddle where houseplants are concerned, but I do grant that the Spider Plant is one of the most neglectable plants you can find. For me, that is virtue enough.

This native of South Africa has foot-long, arching leaves that may remind you of the daylily. Those leaves may be all green but more commonly are striped with cream or yellow. The Spider Plant almost always comes in a hanging basket.

The Spider Plant sends out long runners that eventually droop and trail below the basket. Tiny white flowers appear at the ends of the runners, and then the plantlets develop, usually in the fall and often with several growing off a single stem. In due course, I will tell you exactly what you can do with them.

Light

I've found that bright north light is best for the Spider Plant, but a little sun in the morning or late afternoon is acceptable. Strong, full-day sun is not. Average home or office temperatures are fine for this plant.

Water

The usual twice-a-week regimen is called for to keep the soil evenly moist. If you find, especially in winter, that the soil is still damp midweek, just skip that watering. Too much water may cause the leaves to turn yellow or their tips to turn brown. Browning tips is a common problem with the Spider Plant but nothing to lose sleep over. If it bothers you, trim the tips diagonally, to preserve their shape, with a sharp scissors. If you're in a spraying mood, the Spider Plant is a likely target.

Special Tips

Fertilize regularly in spring and summer. If you have nothing better to do, you might even try propagating the Spider Plant, an easy if idle task. Just snip off a plantlet from its stem, attach with a straight pin to damp soil in a pot, and keep the soil evenly moist. The plant will soon take root and eventually produce its own offspring. You can root several plantlets in the same pot for a fuller effect.

UMBRELLA TREE

This one is sometimes called Australian Umbrella Tree or just plain Umbrella Plant, and just to make matters more confusing, there is another, entirely different genus called Umbrella Plant. To be sure you get what you want, ask for it by the Latin name of *Schefflera*, which has become almost a common name for this plant.

The plant does come from Australia, but why it is called an Umbrella Tree is not so apparent. It may be that its leaflets look something like the spokes of an umbrella, though that takes some stretch of the imagination. My own theory is that if you're ever caught in a shower in an Australian rain forest, the Umbrella Tree, which grows to thirty feet or more there, would be a good thing to take shelter under.

At home, this good-looking plant will grow to four or six feet. The dark green, glossy leaves consist of several smaller leaflets which may be six to eight inches long, spread out like the fingers of your hand. (Now, why didn't they call it the Australian Finger Tree?)

Light

The Umbrella Tree will live in dim light but will thrive in bright. It prefers a little sun or a strong north light, but don't worry if you can't supply them. Do try to keep the plant away from cold windows, which may induce leaf droppage. Average home temperatures are best.

Water

Give your Umbrella Tree a thorough watering on Saturday, or whenever you've decided to do your main watering. Check it midweek, and if the soil is still damp, let it dry out before watering again. You may well find that one watering per week is sufficient, particularly in the winter. Spray and sponge as the spirit moves you.

Special Tips

Feed in the spring with fertilizer spikes if you wish, and prune back if the Umbrella Tree gets too big. Cutting back will help to give you a bushier plant. This plant looks especially good in contemporary settings, either at home or in the office.

AFTERWORD

My friend George says he kills even my fifteen fool-proof houseplants. (You must understand, George is very intellectual.) He claims to have discovered a sixteenth plant that works for him, and I do concede that his solution is practical if rather tacky. I have therefore formulated ELDER'S FIFTH (AND FINAL) LAW: WHEN ALL ELSE FAILS, THINK PLASTIC!